Concrete Mixers

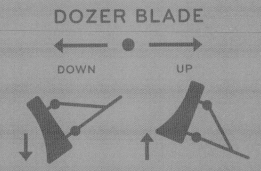

Published by Creative Education

P.O. Box 227, Mankato, Minnesota 56002

Creative Education is an imprint of The Creative Company

www.thecreativecompany.us

Design and production by Rob & Damia Design

Art direction by Rita Marshall

Printed in the United States of America

Photographs by Alamy (Pixonnet.com, qaphotos.com), Corbis,
iStockphoto (Daniel Cardiff, Mike Clarke, Marcel Pelletier, Jim Pruitt,
Paul Vasarhelyi, Jeffrey Zavitski), Damia Stewart/Rob & Damia Design

Library of Congress Cataloging-in-Publication Data

Gilbert, Sara.
Concrete mixers / by Sara Gilbert.
p. cm. — (Machines that build)
Includes index.
ISBN 978-1-58341-726-3
1. Concrete mixers—Juvenile literature. I. Title. II. Series.

TA439.G54 2009
629.225—dc22   2007051659

First edition
9 8 7 6 5 4 3 2 1

CREATIVE EDUCATION

Concrete Mixers

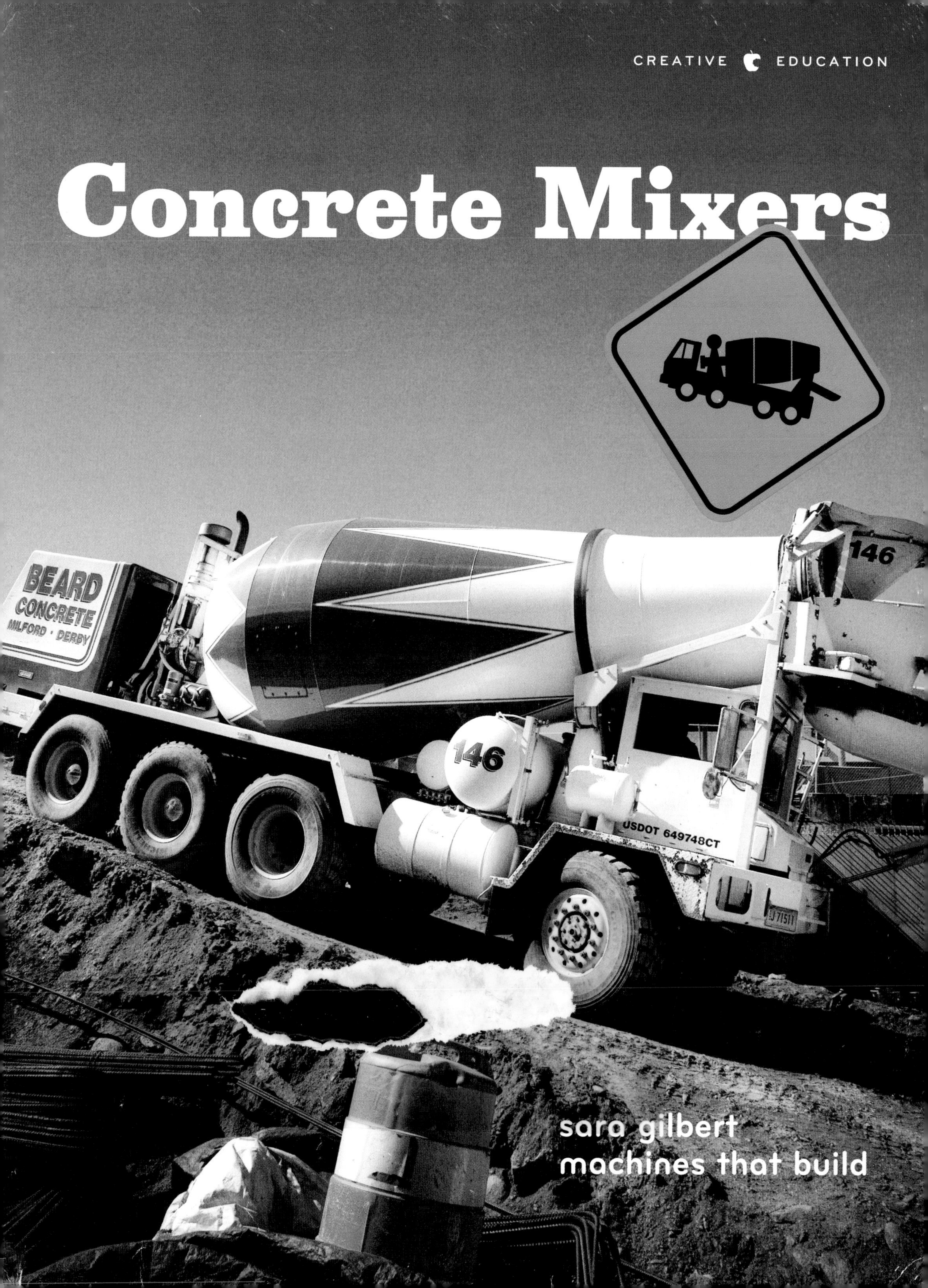

sara gilbert
machines that build

A concrete mixer is a machine that makes concrete. It combines water and cement with sand or gravel. When concrete is inside the mixer, it stays soft. Concrete gets hard when it is poured out and dries.

*Concrete mixers can come
in many different colors.*

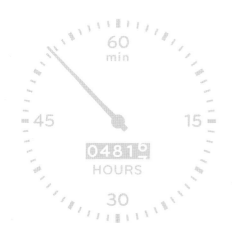

Concrete mixers carry concrete to construction (*con-STRUK-shun*) sites. The concrete spins in a *drum*. Then it is poured out through a *chute*. Workers move the chute so the concrete goes in the right place.

The chute helps move the concrete to the right place.

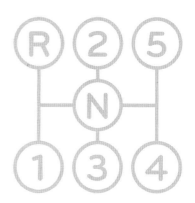

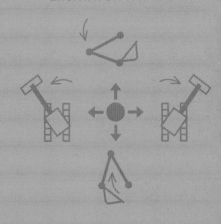

EXCAVATOR PATTERN

Concrete mixers have a cab in front. That is where the *operator* sits. The drum is behind the cab. A blade in the drum stirs the concrete. The blade turns in the opposite direction to pour the concrete.

THROTTLE

Mixers start out clean but can get dirty when in use.

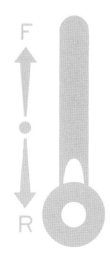

A mixer fills a crane's bucket.

The biggest concrete mixers weigh 30,000 pounds (13.6 t). They can carry up to 40,000 pounds (18 t) of concrete. The drum is so big that it could carry a car!

The mixer operator controls how fast the drum spins.

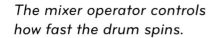

Concrete was first made in the late 1700s. But the first concrete mixer was not built until the early 1900s. The mixer made it easier to make a lot of concrete. People built roads with concrete.

Building a road out of concrete took a long time.

Most concrete mixers have chutes behind the drum. Some mixers have pumps that send concrete from the drum to high places. *Portable* mixers are used for smaller projects.

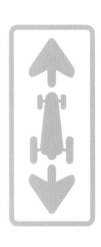

A powerful pump is needed to push concrete up high.

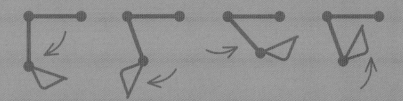

The mixer keeps moving to pour concrete more evenly.

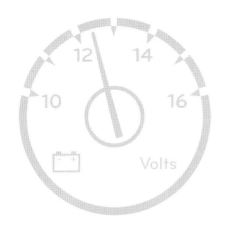

Some concrete mixers have chutes in front of the cab. The operator can watch where the concrete is going. He or she can even move the truck while the concrete is being poured.

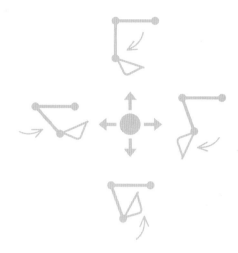

The concrete mixer is loaded through a hole in the top. The water, cement, and gravel are mixed as the truck drives. When the mixer is in the right place, the chute is released.

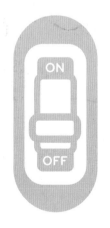

Concrete is sometimes poured
into a shape, or mold.

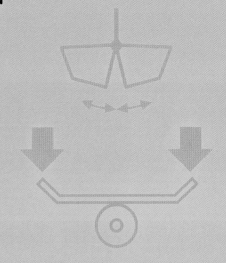

The concrete slides out of the chute quickly. It is pushed out of the drum by the spinning blade. Workers spread the concrete into place. They work fast to smooth it out before it dries!

Workers wear rubber boots and hard hats for safety.

Activity: Be a Mini Mixer

Ask a parent or other grown-up for a small container with a tight lid. Put a small amount of sand and rocks in the container. Then add a little water. Shake it up and roll it around. What happens if you stop moving it? What happens when you dump it out in a bucket?

Glossary

chute: a slide for the concrete that folds down from the front or back of the mixer

drum: a big, round mixer that holds and spins concrete

operator: the person who controls a machine

portable: easy to move and take to different places

Read More About It

Eick, Jean. *Concrete Mixers*. Eden Prairie, Minn.: The Child's World, 1999.

McClellan, Ray. *Concrete Mixers*. Minneapolis: Bellwether Media, 2006.

Index